Geology

Tim Clifford

Rourke

Publishing LLC

Vero Beach, Florida 32964

www.rourkepublishing.com

PHOTO CREDITS: pg 4 © Norman Eder, David Stearn; pg 5 © Mike Morley; pg 6 © Tara Raymo; pg 10 © Malcolm Romain, Steven Tulissi; pg 13 © Clint Scholz, Brian Prawl, Andrea Sturn; pg 14 © Richard Walters; pg 18 © Don Wilkie; pg 19 © Filipe Wiens, Cheryl Seolt; pg 20 © Tanya Costey, David Lewis; pg 21 © Marat Hasanor, P_wei, Tanya Costey, Machenwmedia, Dan Hauser; pg 24 © Wear Adventures; pg 25 © Sherwood Imagery; pg26 © Robert van Beets; pg 27 © Furchin; pg28 © Koch Valérie; pg 29 © Kathy Jones, Armando Tura; pg 33 © Bill Grove; pg 43 © Fire Houe, Linda Bcklin; pg 44 © Jaap Hart, James Phelps.

Editor: Robert Stengard-Olliges

Cover design by Nicky Stratford, bdpublishing.com

Interior design by Renee Brady

Library of Congress Cataloging-in-Publication Data

Clifford, Tim, 1959-
  Geology / Tim Clifford.
      p. cm. -- (Let's explore science)
   ISBN 978-1-60044-623-8
  1. Geology--Juvenile literature. 2. Rocks--Juvenile literature. I. Title.
  QE29.C655 2008
  550--dc22
                                    2007021578

Printed in the USA

CG/CG

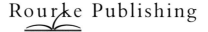

Rourke Publishing

www.rourkepublishing.com – rourke@rourkepublishing.com
Post Office Box 3328, Vero Beach, FL 32964

CONTENTS

CHAPTER ONE

WHAT IS GEOLOGY?

Hells Canyon and Snake River.

The Earth is a fascinating planet, with many incredible features. There are deserts and rainforests, mountains and canyons, and volcanoes and grasslands. How can all these very different features exist on one planet? The study of geology helps us answer this question and more.

Arenal Volcano in Costa Rica.

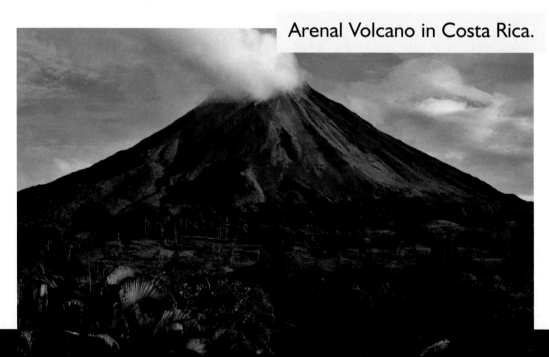

Geologist studying rocks at a dig site.

Geology is the study of the solid matter that makes up the Earth. It includes studying the types of rocks the Earth is made of. Geologists, the scientists who specialize in geology, study many things. They look at how the Earth was formed. They examine how the Earth continues to change over time. Geologists even study rocks to find out what the Earth was like millions of years ago.

CHAPTER TWO

THE EARTH'S LAYERS

The part of the Earth we live on is solid, but the inside of the Earth is very different. Earth has four different layers: the inner **core**, the outer core, the **mantle**, and the **crust**.

The Inner and Outer Core

When the Earth was formed, the heaviest materials sank to the center. These materials formed the Earth's core. They share the same name, but the inner and outer core are very different.

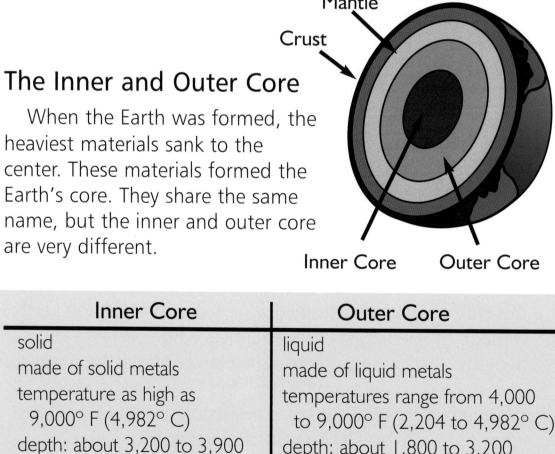

Mantle

Crust

Inner Core

Outer Core

Inner Core	Outer Core
solid	liquid
made of solid metals	made of liquid metals
temperature as high as 9,000° F (4,982° C)	temperatures range from 4,000 to 9,000° F (2,204 to 4,982° C)
depth: about 3,200 to 3,900 miles (5,150 to 6,276 km)	depth: about 1,800 to 3,200 miles (2,897 to 5,150 km)

The Mantle

The thickest part of the Earth is the mantle. It begins about 25 miles (40 km) below the Earth's surface. It reaches 1,800 miles (2,897 km) deep into the Earth.

The mantle is very hot. The parts near the core reach 4,000° F (2,204° C). The parts closest to the Earth's surface reach about 1,600° F (871° C).

The mantle is solid, but the high heat causes the mantle to move slowly beneath the Earth's crust.

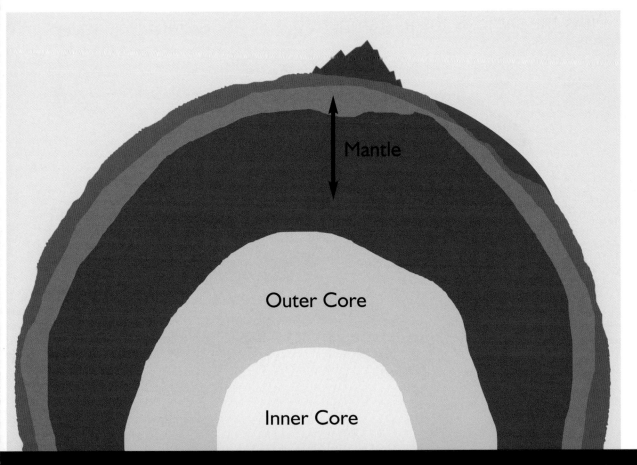

The Crust

We call the outside part of a loaf of bread the crust. We use the same word to describe the outer layer of the Earth. The crust is very thin. It contains less than one percent of the entire volume of the Earth.

There are two types of crust: oceanic crust and continental crust. Oceanic crust lies beneath the oceans and is about five miles (8 km) thick. Continental crust is the rock that makes up the continents. It can range from about 20 to 25 miles (32 to 40 km) thick.

The crust can reach 1,600° F (871° C) near the mantle. It is the same as the air temperature at the surface.

CHAPTER THREE

SOIL

The Lithosphere

Have you noticed that the Earth is hottest at the core and gets cooler as we reach the crust? Because it has cooled, the rock near the Earth's surface is hard and solid. We call this layer of hardened rock the **lithosphere**.

The lithosphere is made up of the crust and upper mantle. Think of it as the layer of solid rock that makes up the hard shell of the Earth. In the same way, the hydrosphere is the water on the Earth's surface. The atmosphere is the layer of gas surrounding the Earth. At the very top of the lithosphere is where we find **soil**.

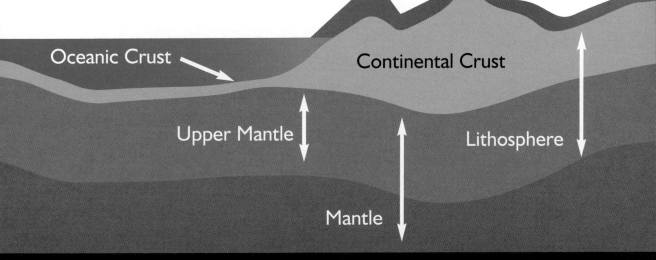

Oceanic Crust

Continental Crust

Upper Mantle

Lithosphere

Mantle

Grass and grass roots in soil.

When people think of soil, they often think of dirt. That's easy to understand, because soil can certainly make you dirty! Soil is very important to life on Earth. It is where plants and grasses grow. It is home to many small animals.

Gopher's make their home in soil.

Just as the Earth has layers, the soil has its own layers. These layers are called **horizons**.

Soil Horizons

Topsoil

Very high in organic matter. Plants grow here. Animals live in and above the topsoil. Can be as much as 12 inches (30 cm) deep.

Subsoil

Lower in organic matter than topsoil. Plant roots often reach down to this level for water. Many nutrients at this level help plants grow. Can range from 6 inches (15 cm) to 3 feet (1 m) below ground.

Weathered Parent Material

Made of rock particles that have been worn down and minerals. Very little life or organic material. Can go many feet deep into the ground.

Bedrock

Solid rock. This layer begins where the weathered parent material ends.

Soil Composition

Soil is made of four different types of material: **organic matter**, **inorganic matter**, air, and water.

Organic matter is the remains and waste of plants and animals. Inorganic matter is non-living matter, such as sand, silt, and clay.

The color of soil is affected by its composition, so geologists can tell a lot about soil from its color.

organic matter

inorganic matter

Think of how sand feels as it squeezes between your toes on the beach. Now think of how clay feels as you mold it. Soil texture is the amount of different sized inorganic particles in the soil. The texture affects how the soil feels when you touch it.

Particle Types and Soil Textures

Sand

The largest sized particle. You can see grains of sand with the naked eye. Sand feels gritty and rough to the touch.

Silt

Smaller sized particles that can only be seen with a microscope. Silt is silky and smooth when wet, and feels almost like flour.

Clay

Particles are much smaller than silt. Clay is sticky when wet and can be easily molded.

Why are some areas of the Earth covered in lush grasslands, while others are barren deserts? Some soils are much more fertile than others. Soil fertility is the soils ability to support plant life.

The type of soil in an area has a great affect on how fertile the soil is. Larger soil particles, like sand, cannot hold water or nutrients very well. That is why the sand in deserts can support very few plants.

The Superstition Mountains in the Arizona desert.

In soil that is made up of silt or clay, water and nutrients stay in the smaller particles. Such soil is much more fertile. Many different types of plants can grow in fertile soil.

Fertile land helps plants grow.

Because of erosion, plants cannot live here.

Soil erosion occurs when wind, rain, or other events move soil from one place to another. This process happens naturally and is part of soil creation. Too much erosion, however, can harm the soil's ability to grow plants.

A soil's color, texture, fertility, and resistance to erosion depend on many things. These include the amount of plant life, leaf cover, root length, rodents, worms, bacteria, and fungi.

CHAPTER FOUR

PLATE TECTONICS

If you think about the size of the continents, it's hard to imagine any of them moving. Yet they do move all the time!

The lithosphere isn't one solid rock. It's broken up into large plates. Scientists believe these huge plates of crust and upper mantle move about on the lower mantle. The theory that the lithosphere is made up of moving plates is called plate tectonics.

The plates move very slowly. The average plate moves no more than about 4 inches (10 cm) a year. Yet, over hundreds of millions of years, the plates have moved long distances. Many scientists believe that continents were once joined but have drifted apart due to **plate tectonics**.

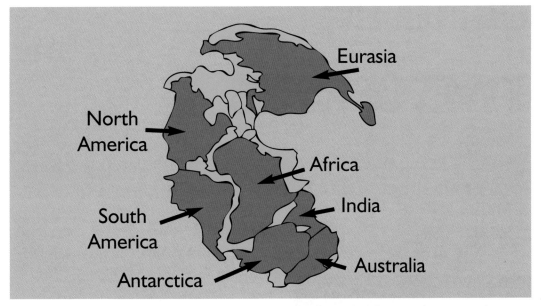

A supercontinent named Pangaea existed on the Earth 250 million years ago.

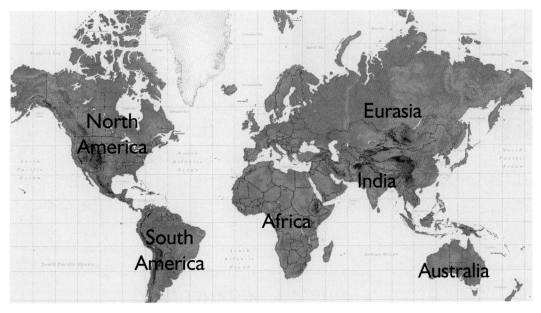

Plate tectonics caused the plates to drift into the positions they occupy today.

CHAPTER FIVE

TYPES OF ROCKS

We all know a rock when we see one. But what makes something a rock? By definition, a rock is a mass of mineral matter.

A **mineral** is a naturally occurring crystalline substance. There are thousands of different types of minerals. Some minerals you may know include salt, coal, copper, quartz, and talc.

A quartz cluster.

Think of rocks as a meal, and the minerals as the ingredients that make up the meal. There are thousands of different ingredients, and different combinations of those ingredients make different meals. In the same way, each rock has its own "ingredient list" of minerals.

All the thousands of different rocks fall into one of three categories: **igneous**, **sedimentary**, and **metamorphic**.

Hot magma river.

Igneous Rocks

We know that the temperatures inside the Earth are very hot. It is so hot that rocks actually turn into a liquid, called magma. This magma can cool beneath the Earth's crust to form igneous rock.

Magma sometimes erupts from the Earth's surface from a volcano. When magma reaches the surface of the Earth, we call it lava. When lava cools, it forms igneous rock.

Common Igneous Rocks

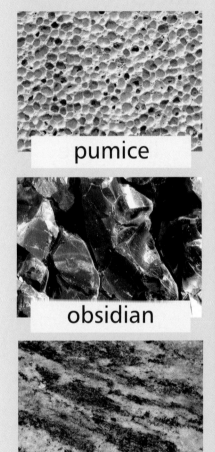

pumice

obsidian

granite

basalt

Common Sedimentary Rocks

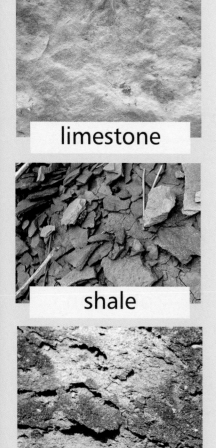
limestone

shale

sandstone

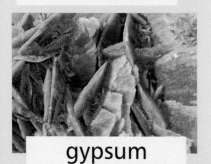
gypsum

Layers of sedimentary rocks.

Sedimentary Rocks

Over time, even something as hard as rock will begin to wear away. When rock wears down, it breaks into much smaller pieces, called **sediment**.

The small pieces of sediment collect together in layers called sediment beds. As the beds get larger, the pressure squeezes the sediment together to form new rock.

Sedimentary rock is new rock formed from the sediment of older rocks.

Metamorphic Rock

A caterpillar changing into a butterfly is an example of metamorphosis. Metamorphosis means to change from one thing into another. Metamorphic rock is rock that has changed from one type of rock to another by pressure or heat. For example, after thousands of years of pressure and heat, limestone is changed into marble.

Metamorphic rocks can be formed from igneous, sedimentary, or even other metamorphic rocks.

Coal can change to a diamond.

Common Metamorphic Rocks

slate

marble

quartzite

soapstone

CHAPTER SIX

LAND FORMATION

You may not realize it, but the land is changing all the time. The Earth is always working to build new land and to wear down the old.

Sometimes changes to the Earth happen rapidly, but other changes can take millions of years!

Processes That Change the Earth

Slow Processes	Rapid Processes
Weathering	Earthquakes
Erosion	Volcanic Eruptions
Deposition of Sediment	Landslides

Constructive Forces

The processes for building new land are called **constructive forces**. Three of the main constructive forces are **crustal deformation**, volcanic **eruptions**, and deposition of sediment.

Crustal deformation occurs when the shape of land (or crust) is changed or deformed. One of the main causes is movement of the Earth's plates. When the plates collide or push toward each other, pressure builds. This can cause two things to happen. The rock can either fold or fault.

Lava covering a road.

Folding

Imagine the tremendous force created when two of the Earth's plates collide! Over time, the pressure can cause rock to fold. When that happens, the rock gets pushed up, and mountains are formed.

Usually, mountains form in ranges, or groups. Some of the best-known mountain ranges are the Himalayas, the Alps, and the Andes. The Rocky Mountains stretch all the way from New Mexico to British Columbia, Canada. That's about 3,000 miles (4,828 km).

View of Mt. Everest, Lhotse and Nuptse from Kala Patthar.

Moraine Park - Rocky Mountain National Park, Colorado.

The San Andreas Fault

The best known fault in North America is the San Andreas Fault. It runs about 800 miles (1,287 km) through California. It was responsible for one of the most famous earthquakes in history, called the Great San Francisco Earthquake of 1906. That earthquake and the fires it caused were one of the greatest natural disasters ever to hit the United States.

Faults

Sometimes, when plates collide, the Earth's crust can crack, or fracture. A fault is formed. Along the crack, or fault line, the rock is being pushed together. Sooner or later, the pressure has to be released. When that happens, the result is an earthquake.

A damaged building after an earthquake.

Magnitude and Effect

1 to 3. Can be recorded, but rarely causes damage. Usually not felt by humans.

3 to 6. Can be felt by humans. Damage is usually minor. Some buildings can be affected.

6 to 9+. Can cause great damage. An earthquake with a magnitude over 6 can cause damage for 100 miles (160 km). Anything greater than 8 can cause severe damage over an area of hundreds of square miles. Earthquakes over 8 only happen about once a year.

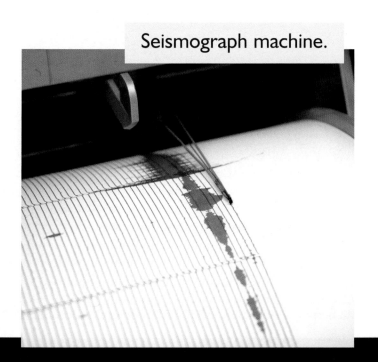

Seismograph machine.

Dr. Charles Richter realized that the shocks caused by earthquakes could be measured. A machine called a seismograph measures the shock, or seismic waves. The magnitude of an earthquake is measured from 1 to 10, with 1 being the smallest and 10 the largest.

Each number on the Richter scale represents a tenfold increase in the strength of the earthquake. An earthquake with a magnitude of 2 is ten times stronger than an earthquake with a magnitude of 1.

Active, Dormant, or Extinct?

Active
A volcano that has erupted in recent history or that is expected to erupt again in the near future.

Dormant
A volcano that has not erupted for a very long time, but may erupt in the future.

Extinct
A volcano that scientists believe will not erupt again.

Volcanic Eruptions

The sight of a mountain pouring out smoke and red hot lava is one of the most amazing in all of nature. A volcano is an opening in the Earth's crust that allows molten rock to escape. This molten rock, or lava, cools after it escapes and becomes igneous rock.

This eruption occurs when pressure forces the release of lava from a volcano.

Eruption in Piton de la Fournaise, Reunion Island.

Mount St. Helens

It started with a series of small earthquakes. They shook Mount St. Helens in Washington State for several months. Steam began to shoot from the top of the mountain. Then, on May 18, 1980, an earthquake with a magnitude of 5.1 caused a collapse of the top of the mountain. Hot magma and ash began gushing out.

Before it was over, 230 square miles (596 sq km) of land were covered in lava and ash. Thousands and thousands of acres were destroyed. Along with thousands of forest animals and millions of fish, 57 people lost their lives.

Mount St. Helens venting steam.

Mount St. Helens from the North Ridge.

Deposition of Sediment

If you could cut into the surface of the Earth, you'd find places where the rock is layered like a birthday cake. These are layers of sedimentary rock, which form when rain, snow, ice, or wind carry rock particles. These particles are deposited in the water.

Over time, a process called **lithification** causes the sediment to turn into sedimentary rock.

Sedimentary rock layers.

Coastline erosion.

Destructive Forces

So far, we've only looked at ways that land is built up. In order for new rocks to be created, older ones must be destroyed.

Land is broken down by **destructive forces**. These forces are at work all the time. Because they work slowly, it is sometimes hard to notice their effect. Without them, however, new rock could never be formed. The two main destructive forces are **weathering** and **erosion**.

Weathering

You might not think that something as harmless as the weather could break down rocks, but it does! Weathering is the breaking down of rocks through exposure to the atmosphere. There are two basic types of weathering: mechanical and chemical.

Mechanical weathering takes place when rocks are broken apart. For example, water in rocks will freeze and thaw based on air temperatures. This causes the water to contract and expand, which weakens the rock. Over time, the rock breaks down.

Chemical weathering causes rocks to weaken. When iron meets water it rusts. The same thing happens to the iron in a rock. When it rusts, or oxidizes, the rock gets weaker, and sooner or later it breaks down.

Iron has oxidized in this rock.

Erosion

Once rocks begin to break down through weathering, erosion can take over. Erosion is the process by which rock particles are moved. Water, wind, ice, and gravity can all cause sediment to break away from rocks.

Usually, particles move from higher places to lower places. Gravity can cause weathered rocks to fall down a mountainside. Rain can wash it into a river, where it moves farther down still. The power of the flow of the river can cause even more sediment to break off along the riverbed.

A rough river can move sediment.

CHAPTER SEVEN

THE ROCK CYCLE

It's hard to think of rocks as moving objects unless you pick one up and throw it! But rocks do move—slowly—as they are created, destroyed, and changed into new types of rock. The way rocks change over time is called the rock cycle.

The rock cycle takes place over a very long period of time. It may take millions of years for a rock to change from one type to another. Understanding the rock cycle can help us understand how the Earth was formed and continues to change.

The diagram on the facing page shows you the entire cycle. Look it over, and then examine each part of the cycle.

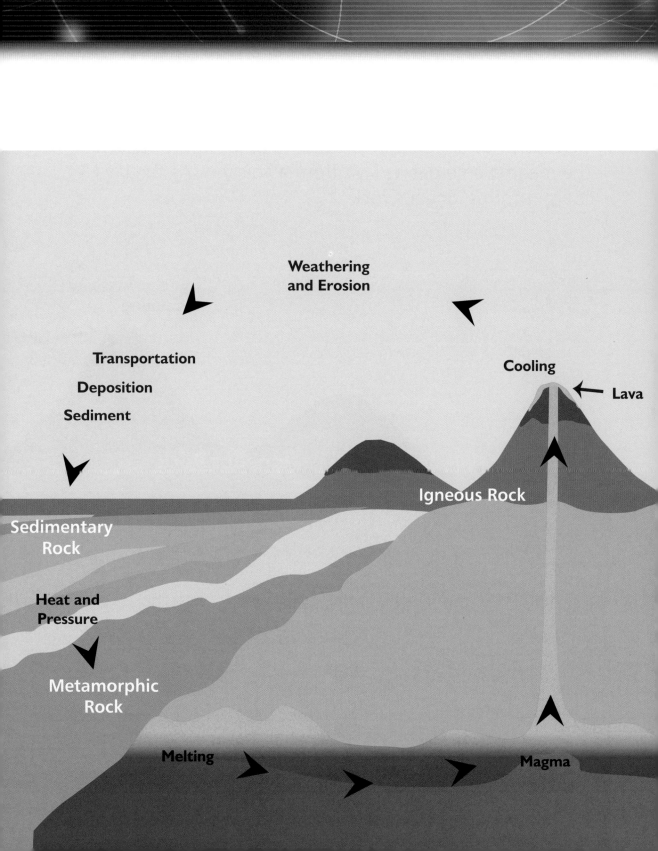

The rock cycle begins far below the Earth's surface. The incredibly hot temperatures cause rock to turn to magma. The magma emerges as lava from a volcano. As the lava cools, it forms igneous rock.

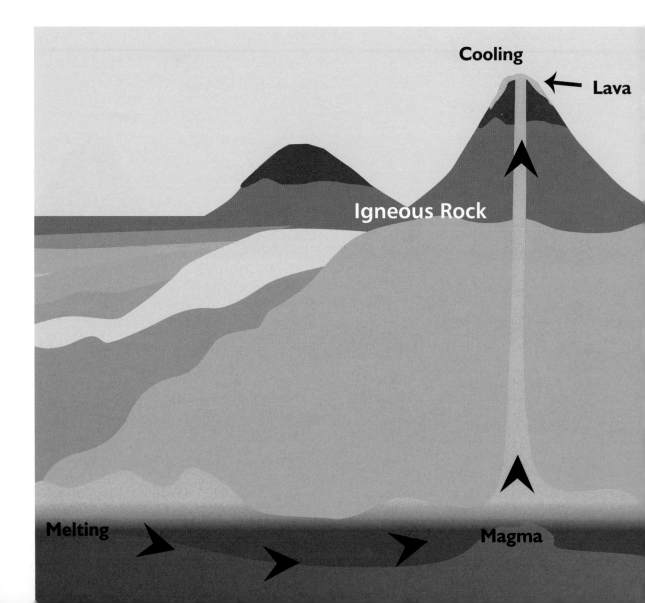

Weathering begins the process of breaking down the igneous rock. Erosion continues the process and transports the sediment along.

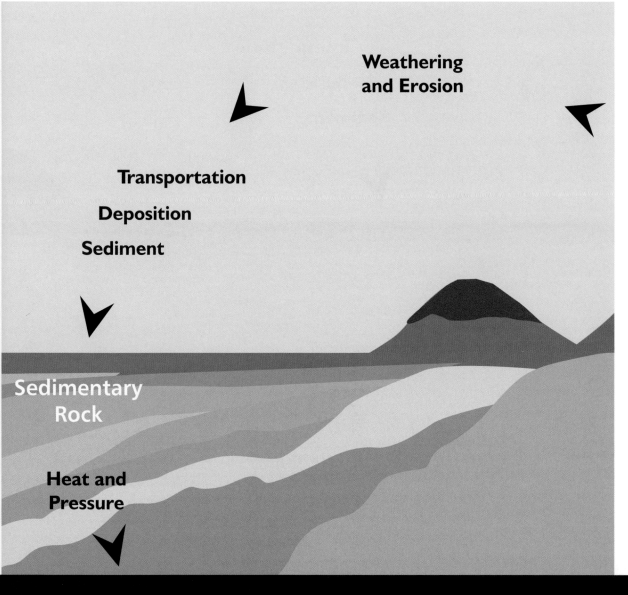

Weathering
and Erosion

Transportation

Deposition

Sediment

Sedimentary
Rock

Heat and
Pressure

Over time, the sediments form sedimentary rock layers at the bottom of rivers, lakes, and streams. Pressure from layer after layer of sedimentary rock causes the rock to change form. Metamorphic rock is created.

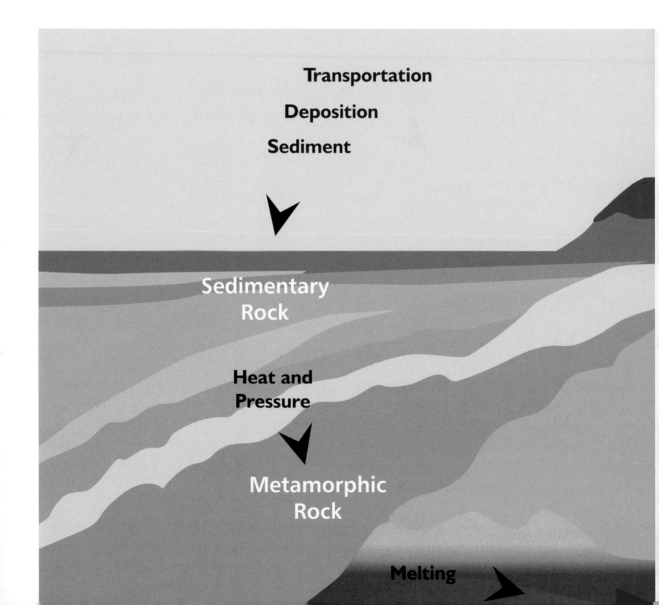

Transportation

Deposition

Sediment

Sedimentary Rock

Heat and Pressure

Metamorphic Rock

Melting

As pressure pushes the rock deeper into the Earth, it heats up and turns into magma. The cycle begins again.

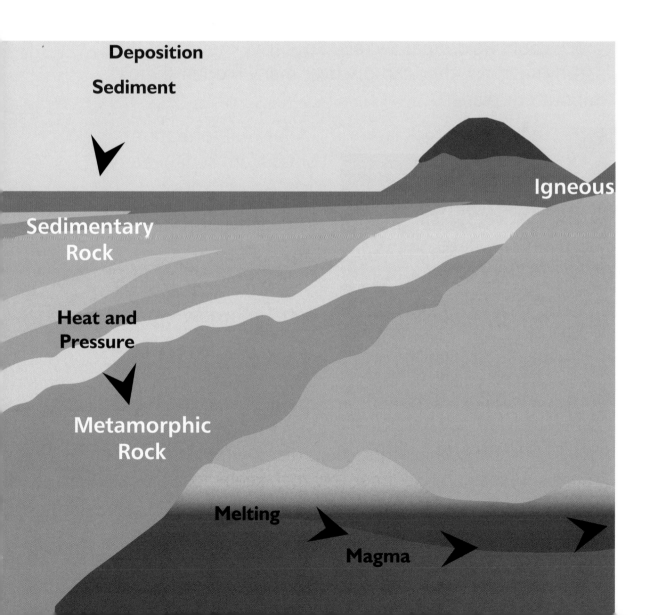

CHAPTER EIGHT

THE SECRETS IN ROCKS

You might not think that something as ordinary as a rock could hold great secrets. Scientists know that by studying rocks, they can discover many hidden things about our planet.

Sedimentary rock layers.

A lot of information comes from sedimentary rock. As you know, sedimentary rock is formed in layers over millions of years. Looking at each layer is like looking at a different period in history.

Sedimentary rock layers are perfect for preserving **fossils**, which are the remains or impressions left in rocks by plants or animals. Metamorphic and igneous rocks destroy fossils with their heat and pressure. Sedimentary rock keeps fossils in good shape.

Fossilization

Fossilization is the process by which an animal or plant becomes a fossil. Here's how a typical dinosaur fossil might be created.

1. A dinosaur dies near water. Its flesh is eaten or decays, leaving only bone.
2. Over time, sediments cover the bones.
3. The layer of sediment turns to rock.
4. The bones turn to minerals.

Dinosaur Extinction

According to the fossil record, it seems that the dinosaurs became extinct, or died off, very rapidly about 65 million years ago.

Many scientists believe that a meteorite 10 miles (16 km) across crashed into the Earth in the Yucatan Peninsula in Mexico at about that same time. Such a collision would have caused massive fires across North America. The darkness from the fires could have blocked the sun and killed off the dinosaurs.

Just how old is the Earth?

Layers of sedimentary rock are deposited over long periods of time. Because of this, the layer in which a fossil is found tells us whether it is older or younger than other fossils.

In 1905, a technique called radiometric dating was discovered. Using this technique, scientists were able to figure out the age of rocks. From there, they were able to calculate the age of the Earth. It is believed that the Earth is about 4.5 billion years old.

Radiometric dating machines.

CHAPTER NINE

AMAZING ROCK FORMATIONS

Take a look at some of the most amazing natural rock formations on Earth!

The Grand Canyon in the western United States is one of the seven natural wonders of the world.

A mesa is a flat area of rock with steep sides. It is caused by erosion.

Hoodoo rocks look like pointed columns rising in the air.

Hickman Bridge, a natural bridge made of rock, is located in Utah.

Questions to Consider

1. Name the three types of rock and describe how each is formed.

2. What factors make it more likely for animals to live where there is silt or clay soil rather than sand?

3. In what ways might the Earth's land change over the next million years? Over the next 100 million years?

Websites to Visit

http://www.pbs.org/wnet/savageearth/

http://www2.nature.nps.gov/geology/tour/

Further Reading

Calson, Mary. *Crumbling Earth: Erosion and Landslides.* Raintree Publishers, 2006.

Lambert, David. *The Field Guide to Geology.* Checkmark Books, 2006.

Morris, John. *The Geology Book Study Guide.* Master Books, 2006.

GLOSSARY

constructive forces (con-STRUK-tiv FORSS) — processes by which rock is created, such as crustal deformation, volcanic eruptions, and deposition of sediment

core (KOHR) — the Earth's center, it is made of an inner core and an outer core

crust (KRUHST) — the outer layer of the Earth

crustal deformation (KRUS-tull dee-for-MAY-shun) — when the shape of land (or crust) is changed or deformed

destructive force (dee-STRUK-tiv FORSS) — processes by which rock is broken down, such as erosion and weathering

erosion (e-ROH-shuhn) — the process by which rock particles are moved

eruption (ee-RUHP-shun) — occurs when pressure forces the release of lava from a volcano

fossils (FOSS-uhls) — the remains or impressions left in rocks by plants or animals

horizons (huh-RIYZ-uhns) — layers of soil

igneous rock (IG-nee-us ROK) — rock formed when magma cools

inorganic matter (IN-or-GAHN-ick MAT uhr) — non-living

matter, such as sand, silt, and clay

lithification (lith-if-ih-CAY-shun) — the process that causes sediment to turn into rock

lithosphere (LITH-oh-sfeer) — a layer of hardened rock made up of the crust and the upper mantle

mantle (MAN-tl) — the thickest part of the Earth that lies just below the crust

metamorphic rock (meht-ah-MORE-fick ROK) — rock that has changed from one type to another by pressure or heat

mineral (MIHN-er-uhl) — a naturally occurring crystalline substance

organic matter (or-GAHN-ick MAT uhr) — the remains and waste of plants and animals

plate tectonics (PLAYT tek-TAH-nix) — the theory that the lithosphere is made up of moving plates

sediment (SED-uh-ment) — small particles of worn away rocks

sedimentary rock (sed-uh-MENT-tuh-ree ROK) — new rock formed from the sediment of older rocks

soil (SOYL) — the thin layer at the very top of the lithosphere consisting of weathered rock and organic matter

soil erosion (SOYL e-ROH-shuhn) — when wind, rain, or other events move soil from one place to another

weathering (WETH-uhr-ing) — the breaking down of rocks

INDEX

About the Author

Tim Clifford is an education writer and the author of several children's books. He is a teacher who lives and works in New York City.